T0065591

Faith to Heal
BREAST CANCER

Just Tara's Touch Pink

authorHOUSE®

AuthorHouse™
1663 Liberty Drive
Bloomington, IN 47403
www.authorhouse.com
Phone: 1 (800) 839-8640

Published by AuthorHouse 09/07/2016

ISBN: 978-1-5246-1845-2 (sc)
ISBN: 978-1-5246-1844-5 (e)

Print information available on the last page.

Any people depicted in stock imagery provided by Thinkstock are models, and such images are being used for illustrative purposes only. Certain stock imagery © Thinkstock.

This book is printed on acid-free paper.

Because of the dynamic nature of the Internet, any web addresses or links contained in this book may have changed since publication and may no longer be valid. The views expressed in this work are solely those of the author and do not necessarily reflect the views of the publisher, and the publisher hereby disclaims any responsibility for them.

Scripture quotations marked KJV are from the Holy Bible, King James Version (Authorized Version). First published in 1611. Quoted from the KJV Classic Reference Bible, Copyright © 1983 by The Zondervan Corporation

Table of Contents

1   Introduction ix

2   Acknowledgments.. xi

3   Courage...1

4   My Journey with Fighting Breast Cancer In My
    Own Words 2

5   Hope..7

6   Strength 13

7   Faith..27

8   Believe 50

9   Love...51

10 References..57

About Me... The Author...Just Tara 59

CANCER PREVENTION

INTRODUCTION

BREAST CANCER

Breast Cancer is the
Restoring of your body
Every day with God's
Assurance of a brand new
Self changing appearance that when done you will have a
Testimony that you had cancer and that
Cancer was just
Another
Name for
Christ's
Ever loving way of
Restoring of your Mind, Body, and Soul to clean out the old
you and bring on the new you for a testimony of GOD'S
healing powers

FOR IN CHRIST YOU ARE A NEW CREATURE...
OLD THINGS ARE PASSED AWAY AND
ALL THINGS BECOME NEW AGAIN....

This is what Breast Cancer was for ME.....
So I announce to the world:

JUST TARA'S TOUCH PINK....

"TOUCH PINK"
Touching
Others
Using my
Cancer
Healing for
People
In
Need of
Knowledge about Breast Cancer...

ACKNOWLEDGMENTS

First and foremost, I would like to thank God. For, without him I would not be here to write this book or my thank you notes. It is all because of God that I still live, move, and have my being. I love you God!!!!

I would like to thank my mother, Betty Booker for always being there for me and instilling the love of God in me at an early age. Thanks to my father, Johnny Stephens for always standing by my side through anything.

I would like to thank my daughter, D'Ara for giving me a reason to press on and to fight to live through breast cancer so she could continue to have a mother in her life.

I would like to thank Ricoe L. Paul for always being there for me and loving me through my breast cancer fight. I would also like to thank him for taking care of me and my sick mother. He did everything for us and I will always love you for that and I mean it from the bottom of my heart.

Thanks to all families and friends who prayed for me in my time of sickness. I love you Teresa Ann McClendon and Juandolyn "Jay" Kashiri my two best friends in the whole world. My sisters thanks for your listening ears.

Thanks to the Clifford Grove Baptist Church Family, Macedonia Baptist Church Family, and all the churches for praying for me and my family in my time of sickness.

Thanks to my cousins Janette Smith and Joyce Smith for being here for us (me, mom, and D'Ara) when we needed you all the most.

Special thanks also to Joyce Smith, who helped me to complete this book. I will always love you cousin. You are the sister I never had. To Celest Ngeve, for also helping me to complete this book. I love you my Sista Cypha. To Michelle White Cofer, thanks for your editing skills. I love you girl!! To Doris and Darnell Thomas thanks for taking care of our baby D'Ara while I was fighting Breast Cancer. I love you both!! Last, but not least Pastor Randy Templeton thanks for coming into my life and helping me to put the final touches to this book and make everything happen in God's timing.

God Bless You All!!!

1

COURAGE

I put on my fighting clothes once diagnosed with Breast Cancer. I had the courage of a lady waiting to go to war. The slogan says "fight like a girl." I didn't know all this was in store. I had the courage of Ruth as she did when she was left alone. She knew her Boaz would come one day.

I knew the inner courage would carry me all the way to the end. And sure enough it did. I beat Breast Cancer because I had the COURAGE to "fight like a girl" all the way to the end.

2

MY JOURNEY WITH FIGHTING BREAST CANCER IN MY OWN WORDS

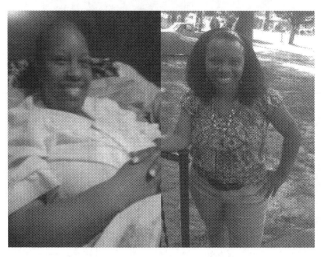

I first started getting lumps in my breasts at the age of 15, when my menstrual cycle started. The lumps would appear in both breasts and go away once my menstrual cycle stopped. I informed my gynecologist about a lump nine years ago after I had my daughter, D'Ara. The gynecologist told me, "oh no this lump is not cancer, just a fibroid cyst." At that time, I did not do a mammogram or anything. He completed a Breast Exam on me and I would do monthly BSE, breast self exams. In July 2008, I noticed a big lump in my right breast that I could clearly see and feel. It hurt so bad that I couldn't sleep at night. I had to place pillows on my breast, where the lump was, in order to sleep at night.

I made a doctor's appointment with Dr. Dennis to check on it after a car accident in August 2008. Dr. Dennis was busy that day so I had to see Dr. Harris. She was the new female doctor in Washington, Georgia. She checked me out and told me that the lumps in my breast felt like they were 2 to 3 centimeters and she wanted to put me on medicines to see if the lumps would disappear. She prescribed Cephalexin for 10 days.

I took the medicine as prescribed, but the pain continued. I returned to see Dr. Harris at this visit, she stated that I needed further testing since the medicine didn't help. She ordered me an ultrasound and a mammogram for my breasts at a Breast Health Center in Athens, Georgia.

I took my first mammogram and ultrasound on 9-10-2008, at the Breast Health Center in Athens, Georgia. The results from those tests came back indicating abnormalities in my right breast. They reported I needed to have an ultrasound biopsy done on my right breast to check for cancer. I had the biopsy done on 9-16-2008. I was very nervous getting this done, but I made it through.

I received the dreaded phone call from Dr. Harris on 9-17-2008 around 1:00 p.m. and she said that I had BREAST CANCER in my right breast. I immediately cried and told my mom. She told me not to worry and that God would take care of me. I then told my best friends Teresa "Ann" and Juandolyn "Jay." They consoled me, told me that everything would be alright, and that they had my back. I said, "BUT GOD!!!!" I was worried and had crying spells, but I know that I know that I knew God is Able!!! I called my church family and other family members and told them the news also. My church family said they'd pray with me for my healing.

I received the news of being diagnosed with Breast Cancer at the age of 34. I had to start making preparations to visit the cancer doctor, chemotherapy doctor, and to get a Medicaid card. Initially, I got the run around about my doctor's appointments. I was scared and also angry for having to wait so long to see a doctor. I completed the Medicaid card paper work. I made my first oncology (Surgeon) appointment for 10-1-2008 to see Dr. Gilbert. Dr. Gilbert was the doctor my cousin told me about. So on 10-1-2008, I went to see him.

Dr. Gilbert told me that my Breast Cancer was very treatable. He told me of my options: surgery, chemotherapy, or do nothing. He said he wanted to try and save my whole right breast. He advised that having chemotherapy first, would be best for me. He said I would do chemotherapy, surgery, and then radiation therapy. He wanted to see if the chemotherapy would reduce the lump down so I wouldn't have to have extreme surgery on my breast. He told me that chemotherapy is different for everyone, and I would need to focus on myself and how my body would react to it. He cautioned me not to listen to other people's story, but to focus on my story. He set up an appointment for chemotherapy with Dr. Valdo (Medical Oncologist) on 10-3-2008.

On 10-3-2008, I met with Dr. Valdo at the Cancer Care Center in Athens, Georgia. Dr. Valdo examined me and told me that he felt like I could beat this cancer. Since my veins are small and hard to find, I had to have a port placed in my arm to get the chemotherapy medicine that I needed to get better.

Sometime in October 2008, I went to D'Ara's school; when she was in 4th grade and I spoke to the class about my Breast Cancer. The class was discussing Cancer and Cancer Awareness Month. D'Ara's class was concerned that she would get Breast Cancer so she asked me to come and share with her class. I educated the class on my experience with Breast Cancer. I answered the class's questions to the best of my knowledge and ability. The class was very inquisitive about my situation. I assured them that neither they nor D'Ara could "catch" Cancer from me. They were so surprised to see me happy and eager to share my experience. My visit with the class helped the children understand the feelings D'Ara was having and they were more understanding to her and how her family was being affected with this thing called Cancer.

Dr. Gilbert spoke with me also about getting a Breast MRI done before my port placement. I had the Breast MRI done 10-9-2008 at the Imaging Building in Athens, Georgia. I was very, very, very scared about getting this MRI procedure done. I thought that I had to be enclosed in the MRI machine. Praise God it was an OPEN MRI BREAST SCAN MACHINE. I was praising God and quoting scriptures as the procedure was being done. I am healed by his stripes. I was up high on the MRI machine. I could see down through the machine.

I could hardly breathe in the machine, but God!!!

On 10-10-2008, I had my first class on chemotherapy. They discussed what it is and how many treatments I had to have and how it may or may not affect me. I had to have a total of 8 chemotherapy treatments: four of Adriamycin & Cytoxan (A & C) and four of the T (TAXOL) treatments. As I took the treatments, I learned when I was eligible for surgery to remove the lumps. The nurse, Ms. Keona, was very nice and sweet. She spoke honestly with me on the basics for chemotherapy. She also told me to focus on me, my story, and my body for chemotherapy.

On 10-11-08, we celebrated my boyfriend's (Ricoe L. Paul) 35th birthday. We ate out at a restaurant, shopped at outlet stores in Commerce, Georgia, and took family portraits at a portrait studio. We had a great time celebrating his birthday.

On 10-12-2008, an old friend gave me a nice card and $20.00. I was very thankful and Happy!! Amen!!

On 10-13-2008, I had to get my port put in my left arm and I also had to have a heart muga scan done at a hospital in Athens, Georgia. My mom and my cousin took me to the hospital. While at the hospital, I was given some medicine called Versed and Fentanyl to help sedate me, but I had an allergic reaction to it. I itched really, really, bad and the nurses had to give me some Benadryl and more medicine to help sedate me again so I could get the procedure done. I itched on my head, my hands, and my legs. My neck, stomach, and my back turned RED from the medicine.

I stayed at the hospital from 8:00 a.m. to 3:00 p.m. The procedure was okay except for my reaction to the medicine. I prayed to God when I was getting all of the medicine. God helped me through this and I knew he'd help me as I began my chemotherapy treatments. God is my healer; the battle is his, not mine!!!!! I am healed by his stripes!!!!! Praise God!!!!

HOPE, FAITH, LOVE, AND COURAGE…..FIGHT FOR THE CURE…..CANCER…..BREAST CANCER…

3

HOPE

I am a picture of hope at its finest.

I have lived through my hope.

Hope to me is what you want in the future.

I had a vision of hope in my breast cancer struggles.

My hope was to: Help Others Persevere Even (in my own sickness).

I knew my sickness was to help others see JESUS through my going through.

I offer HOPE to the nation in my journey with fighting Breast Cancer.

On 10-14-2008, I was supposed to start my first chemo treatment, but after reviewing my MRI results another lump and lymph nodes were found in my right breast and arm again. BUT GOD!!!! I was nervous and anxious, but I knew all things happen for a reason. Two days later I had to go back to the Breast Health Center to get ultrasounds and biopsies done on these areas found! I knew God would see me through again!!! D'Ara was sick today with a headache and she's vomiting. I knew she'd be okay, too, by the grace of God!!! I told God, "God I know you're doing something in this... I love you, I praise you, and I know you're working it out for my good!" Amen!!!!

I went to the Cancer Care Center to get the needle removed out of my port today. It hurt a little bit. The nurse changed the needle and the dressing over the port. D'Ara was only dehydrated. Praise God!! The doctor said D'Ara needed some counseling about my diagnosis with Breast Cancer. I am going to get D'Ara enrolled in counseling so that she can understand what I am facing and fighting. We will undergo counseling together so that we can both understand how to cope with all of this.

On 10-15-08, I went to the Radiology department at the hospital to have my port placement re-dressed again. The nurse said it looked fine and wasn't infected. She redressed it and I went home. I called Dr. Gilbert to check on the counseling session, for D'Ara and me, at the Center for Cancer Support. Dr. Gilbert agreed to send a referral for these services and we should hear something soon. I was feeling okay today and D'Ara was better also. I was so happy!! God is able and I began preparing for tomorrow's visit at the Breast Health Center. I know the results will be negative for Cancer this time around. God is my Healer!!!

On 10-16-08, I had an appointment for another right breast ultrasound. I had to get another biopsy done on my breasts. The lymph nodes were tested to be negative for cancer. Praise God Almighty!! The other lump looked suspicious so it had to be biopsied. This procedure was done by Dr. Screven!! She helped me through this again! Mom, D'Ara, Tree, Maverick, and I went to an Italian restaurant to eat out. We had fun eating and hanging out at the restaurant, then going to the Athens Mall.

On October 17, 2008, and I became very sick. I was nauseated, my breasts were hurting, my head was hurting, and I could barely move. Ricoe had to help me get dressed. I hoped that this was not due to the procedure I had on the day before. Momma took me back to the Breast Health Center to check on my breasts. Nurse Maria, who I met yesterday, examined me. She said my breast was okay and that the port in my arm was okay also. She thought that I had the 24 hour virus that was going around. She told me to go home and take my nausea and diarrhea medicines and I should feel better by tomorrow. I came home and took my medicines as told. After taking the medicine, I felt a little better! I had to wait 3-5 days to find the results of the 2nd biopsy. BUT GOD!!!!! Also on today, D'Ara's mentor took her on an outing and they came back with two nice cards of encouragement. I wanted to cry. The cards were so sweet... actually, I did cry.

10-19-08, Momma gave me a nice card that encouraged me to get well. It was very sweet and I wanted to cry again. I know that my momma and D'Ara have my back and are praying for me. My cousin in Rayle cooked for me today: neck bones, rice, and tomatoes. It was Umh Umh good!!!

10-27-08, I went to the Cancer Care center for an appointment.....I thought. After arriving there, I was told I was starting my first chemotherapy treatment. I was a little scared and anxious, but glad to be starting treatment. I stayed there nearly 6 hours. I had a room by myself. The treatment went fine on the first day. After getting home, I was tired, nauseated, and my whole body hurt. I went through a change like no other. My taste buds went away, my skin changed colors, and my fingernails grew, and turned blue. I was told I'd have treatments every two weeks. I couldn't eat anything without throwing up!!! My sex drive went away also!!! I was in a state of surprise at all of this happening.

Tuesday, 10-28-08, I had to go back to the Cancer Care Center to get a Neulasta shot. I will have to get these shots every Tuesday after each chemotherapy treatments. The shots made me feel more nauseated and even sicker. The doctors felt that the chemotherapy was making me sick, not the shot. However, I found myself feeling sicker after the shots instead of after chemotherapy!!

11-10-08, was the day of my second treatment. I was in a room with other people. This treatment took nearly four hours. This time I had to get fluids. I was so sick. My nurse, Ms. Geana, helped me out a lot. She made sure I was feeling okay before I left to go home.

11-23-08, this is the day that my baby D'Ara and her cousin got baptized at Church. I was so happy that my baby was saved and accepted the Lord Jesus Christ as her personal savior. We all helped share in her special day. Also on today, the men (MOV – Men of Vision) of "The Grove" fed us our Thanksgiving Dinner. It was delicious! We were being served hand and foot. Ha!!! Ha!!! Thank you Jesus!!!!

11-24-08, I had treatment number three. It was a hard treatment also. My hair was starting to fall out from taking the chemotherapy treatments. I went to the Barber shop and Patrick cut my hair down low for me. Later, Ricoe cut all my hair for me. **My HAIR IS GONE from ALL OVER MY BODY:** private parts, head, and all. I received the shots as usual and also more fluids. I had to get fluids for two days (Tuesday and Wednesday). I was so sick. Once again, "Mama Geana" my nurse took great care of me. Mama Geana and Geasha made sure I was able to travel for Thanksgiving.

On Wednesday, 11-26-08, we traveled to Hardeeville, South Carolina (Ricoe's mother's house) for Thanksgiving. I felt really tired, but better to travel. I met Ricoe's family that Wednesday night and Thursday morning. Momma and D'Ara also came. Ricoe and I stayed at the hotel. Mom and D'Ara stayed at Ricoe's mother's house. I really had no taste for food at all. My body hurt and I felt very bad. Thanksgiving Day, 11-27-08, dinner was at Mama Shirley's house. I met Ricoe's other family members today also. Thanksgiving night at the hotel, I had a bad night. I cried all night long because I felt bad, physically, all over my whole body. Ricoe helped me get through it though. He made me feel like everything was still going to be okay even though I was sick. Thank God for Ricoe!!!! We went to the Shrimp House Restaurant and I ate a lot of fresh shrimp. My taste buds had returned a little. We visited various stores and rode around Savannah, Georgia, site seeing, on Friday and Saturday. We rode through the River Walk in Savannah and went to the flea market. While site seeing in Savannah, we saw horse carriages. We saw the big bridge in Savannah, as well.

Sunday, 11-30-08, was a bad day. I had a very bad crying spell and it hit me hard because I could not eat anything like normal. We were at a chicken restaurant where my mom, D'ara, and Ricoe were eating though I couldn't. It made me feel sad and it really bothered me. I also had an accident for the first time; I messed up my clothes because I didn't make it to the restroom in time. I had to change my clothes. This made me feel so embarrassed!!!!

Also while in Hardeeville, I had vaginal problems occur. My vaginal area started hurting that Saturday. So on that Monday, 12-1-08, I went to the doctor to see what was wrong. The doctor told me that I had a vaginal urinary tract infection (UTI) due to using the water at the hotel in South Carolina. The water was brown and dirty at the hotel and had broken me out. I was very sick!!! The doctors prescribed me an antibiotic medicine for the infection. I came home from the doctor, took the medicine, and I passed out after I was taking a shower. I was out for about 2 or 3 minutes. I got up off of the floor and went to bed! It felt like I was about to DIE! I WAS SO SCARED! I told the doctor about the medicine and so they gave me cream instead of taking pills for the UTI. This was very complicated for me. I was already sick with breast cancer now this.....gods help me make it through. **Lord I am calling for your STRENGTH RIGHT NOW!!! I NEED YOU LORD GOD... GIVE ME THE STRENGTH TO FIGHT THIS BATTLE OF CANCER AND THIS INFECTION SATAN HAS BROUGHT TO MY BODY.**

4

STRENGTH

Do you have enough strength to fight this battle I often asked myself?

Tired of being stuck with needles, tired of taking medicines, tired of crying

Tired of panic attacks, tired of going to the doctors, tired of hospitals

Sick and tired of being sick and tired

But.....

I found strength in God and in his Holy word.

"My strength is made known in your weakness," says God.

"When you're weak that is when I am strong"

"The strong bears the infirmities of the weak."

"I am more than a conqueror through Christ Jesus."

"By his stripes I am healed."

"I can do all things through Christ who strengthens me."

I know that you are with me and I thank you God for your undying love and this thing called **STRENGTH.**

12-08-08, I had treatment number four. This was the last of the A & C treatments. I was very happy. The A & C treatments made me very nauseated and very sick. I was sick for the whole week (12-8-08 to 12-13-08). I was in the bed the whole week and I could not move. I took the Neulasta shot as usual. My spirit was low. **I THOUGHT I WAS NOT GOING TO MAKE IT THROUGH.** I didn't feel like doing anything!!! I lay in my bed crying and praying to GOD to heal me and to pull me through this Breast Cancer. I was watching the gospel channel (14) on television, when a minister and his wife began speaking on **praying for someone else (so you can be healed) they discussed James 5:16.** It was then that I knew that I went through this breast cancer illness so that others could be healed, when they witness how God healed me. I cried out to God. I prayed for people to pray for me so my healing could really begin to come forth. As I began to pray, my family members and church family members came to mind. I prayed for them and a little girl who I saw on television that also had cancer.

I forced myself to get out of bed on 12-13-08 to go to the WOW (Women of Worship) annual, end- of- year gala. It was at my church in Rayle, Georgia. Minister Bernice was the speaker. She spoke on <u>"Beauty for Ashes"</u> from Isaiah 61:1-3. The song "Let Go, Let God" was played. She also talked about having a REAL RELATIONSHIP WITH GOD!!

Evangelist Lois had spoken with me earlier this week on the same thing. This was my confirmation from God. I was totally amazed and in awe! Minister Bernice and First Lady Rochelle prayed for me and my healing. I felt the Holy Spirit all over my body and I felt 100% better after I left, than I had when I first got there. The devil thought he had me, **BUT GOD!!!** GOD pulled me through again by using his vessel Minister Bell. At that time, Minister Bernice did not know that I had Breast Cancer. She prayed all over my whole entire body!! It was like I never hurt... PRAISE GOD!!! THANK YOU JESUS!!!! I was truly inspired and uplifted as she spoke. It was much needed, to help me cope with all I was going through at this time in my life. She told us to let our relationship with Jesus be real and not fake. She told us that Jesus is our healer. It is so, Amen!!!!!

MY 35th BIRTHDAY PARTY!!!

12-14-08---- AT HOME IN ATHENS, GEORGIA----

I was energized again!!! Mom and Ricoe gave me my 35TH BIRTHDAY PARTY, though my Birthday is actually DECEMBER 17TH. The party was very sweet and filled with good fun. Lots of family and friends came and said good words of encouragement to me. Ricoe cooked a good dinner for my party. I received a necklace from Ricoe, smell good lotions from Lisa, $10.00 and a card from Georgiamae, $1.35 from Mr. Uncle Ozzie. (LOL) "It's a family tradition he does every year $1.00 gold coin and the change for each yr old I am." Party attendees: Mom, Ricoe, D'Ara, Frank, Georgiamae, Pearl, Jenny, Tika, Evangelist Perlotte, Johnnie, "Mr." Uncle Ozzie, Zan, William Booker, Doris Thomas, Gena Davis, Destini Jennings, Marae, Raisa, Macie, Leemarcus, Tony, and Cullen. We had a great time at my birthday party.

MY 35TH BIRTHDAY!!!!

My 35th BIRTHDAY was 12-17-08 and my friend Cheryl took me out for lunch at an Italian Restaurant. I was not feeling the best, but I thanked God to have been alive. She called me earlier in the month to check on me and we decided we'd go out to celebrate my birthday. She really encouraged me to hang on in there and to fight this thing called Cancer.

On 12-19-08, I spoke about my Breast Cancer at Macedonia Baptist Church for their Women's Conference. It went very good. My hope was to encourage some ladies to go get a mammogram and get checked for Breast Cancer. I spoke about my challenges, so far, as I had dealing with breast cancer. All praises go to God Almighty!!!!

12-22-08 was treatment day number five. I started the new medicines today, Taxol treatments. This treatment was very rough. I received the medicines Zofran and Benadryl. It almost killed me. I was SO, SO, SO, SO, SCARED. I was shaking all over my whole body. My heart rate read at 133 beats a minute. I could not see anything.

Something in the back of my mind kept telling me not to go to sleep or close my eyes. I was very sleepy from the Benadryl medicine. I just kept quoting scriptures to myself and saying that **I MUST LIVE FOR MY DAUGHTER D'ARA!!** I said to myself "no weapon formed against me shall prosper, you shall live and not die, you are healed by his stripes, and pray ye one for another that you may be healed….." I barely saw nurse Penelope walk by, yet I called out to her for help. She came up to me and stopped the medicines. She got other nurses to help her. She called for Nurses Patricia, Pearl, and intern nurse Laurena to assist her. They all began to work on me. I could not stop shaking and speaking in a slurred speech. I kept on asking if I was going to be alright and if I was going to live through this. The nurses assured me that I would be okay. The nurses said I was having a Panic Attack. I did not know what was going on. **I WAS JUST SCARED TO DEATH!!!! I SURELY THOUGHT IT WAS GOING TO BE OVER FOR ME AGAIN!!!!** The nurses gave me more medicine to get me back where I needed to be.

This week was a rough week also. Christmas Day, 12-25-08, I spent mostly in the bed after D'Ara opened up her gifts and went to her dad's house. I played with her for a little while and then back to bed. I was not feeling good at all. December was also a month where I started to get hemorrhoids very bad!!! I tried to fix it with suppositories, creams, pads, and all. I got no justice from them… My doctor says it's all the **CHEMOTHERAPY…. I STILL PRAYED GOD HELP ME TO GET THROUGH THIS!!!!! AMEN!!!!!!!**

HAPPY NEW YEAR ….
THANK GOD I MADE IT
ANOTHER YEAR….2009

1-5-09 was treatment number six. I was still on Taxol treatments. The nurses at the center tried to give me Zofran again, but **I WOULD NOT TAKE IT** after what happened last time. I took Benadryl in a pill form this time. I was still sleepy during this treatment, but not like last time. I got nauseated while taking my treatment. My bones have started to hurt since taking my treatments number five and six. I burned a lot this time also. My face and arm tingled where the port was in my arm. I feel I turned yellow from this, but the nurse says my skin just lightened up. I was scared that I had yellow jaundice. I asked the nurse and she confirmed that I didn't. The medicine made me brighter and lightened up my skin. These are some of the changes my body was going through:

- ❖ **Tiredness**
- ❖ **Spitting A lot**
- ❖ **Bones Hurting**
- ❖ **Hair Loss**
- ❖ **Hemorrhoids**
- ❖ **Eye brows and Eye Lashes Falling Out**
- ❖ **Skin Burning**
- ❖ **Dry Skin**
- ❖ **Menstrual Cycle – went away –**
- ❖ **Teeth Chipping and Gums Bleeding a lot**
- ❖ **Constant Nausea**
- ❖ **Diarrhea**
- ❖ **Blurred Vision**

1-12-2009, I went to a make up class that helps u look good… and feel better at the Cancer Center. It was really fun. I met a lot of new people who are fighting this thing called CANCER. On 1-13-09, D'Ara and I went to talk with Lissete, the Social Worker. She helped D'Ara and I understand a little more of what I am going through. She really made it a little clearer for me. I think

D'Ara will be fine now that she knows medically what I am going through. **<u>PRAISE GOD!!!</u>**

1-19-2009, I had treatment #7, still on Taxol treatments. This treatment went okay. I was scared because lately all the medicines I received have made me sick or feel faint. I thank God that I made it through this treatment without any problems.

2-2-2009, Treatment #8, I was supposed to have my 8th and final treatment on today. Unfortunately, I had Another panic attack and was scared frantically. The medicines had me going crazy! I didn't want anymore medicines at all. I cried, I felt my heart going all over the place I had to leave the center.

It was a rainy day; a friend picked me up from the Center after not taking my treatment. We had a car wreck 2 minutes from the house. We were hit in the rear. This made me feel even worse than when I was at the Center. I walked home in the rain. Ricoe met me at the top of the hill. I was shaken up all day and night long.

My heart raced and raced. About twelve midnight, my Momma Betty and Doris took me to the emergency Room. They checked my heart, my blood pressure, and my vital signs. I stayed connected to an EKG machine for four hours. They said the steroids had me anxious and nervous. I went home and tried treatment #8 again the next day.

2-3-2009, FINALLY, TREATMENT #8

I was still scared and overwhelmed from yesterday and last night. I didn't want anymore Decadron. Nurse K came to talk with me, but I didn't want to hear her. I was the one feeling like I was going to die because my heart was racing. I was tired and felt like giving up. But, Momma "Geana" and Momma "Penelope" told me not to worry; they helped me through it. They ensured that I had a private room and getting me an anxiety shot (Ativan) to finish my last treatment. So nurse "Fayena" came in and prayed with me and gave me my last treatment and the next thing I knew it was over!! **Praise God!! CHEMOTHERAPY...done and over with...Thank You Lord!!!**

D'Ara, Doris, her friend Kennae and I went to a PINK OUT Basketball Game in Athens, Georgia for Breast Cancer Awareness on 2-8-2009. We had mad fun, but I wasn't feeling my best. I pressed my way to the game anyway to have fun with D'Ara. We ate lunch, took pictures and I did the survivors walk on the court. D'Ara, Kennae, and Doris cheered me on. All of the breast cancer survivors had fun on the court as well. We met the basketball players and the mascot. D'Ara, Kennae, and Doris enjoyed themselves.

On March 3, 2009 my mom had a double by-pass heart surgery procedure done. I was very scared considering what I was already facing. The devil sure was busy trying to steal my joy and happiness by attacking my body and my momma's body....**BUT GOD**... It snowed for one whole week in Athens, Georgia. The snow was 3 to 4 inches. Ricoe and I had kept warm in my momma's new van she bought. We had no lights for 2 days. But by God's grace and mercy we still made it.... snow and all... Thank you Jesus!!!

I went back to the Cancer Center for a follow up appointment to see when I would have my surgery done! In the meantime, I found a lump in my left breast. I was worried about it so I called Dr. Gilbert to schedule a mammogram to get it checked out. Dr Gilbert scheduled the mammogram for me. My cousin Jan and I went on March 5, 2009, for our mammograms. The mammogram hurt but I had to get it done. While I was there, I had another biopsy done. I cried because I was still scared as to what was going on with me and my body. **While we were there the building caught on fire, we had to exit the building for 5 or 10 minutes. Satan is busy but GOD!!** We returned back to the building safely and I had my biopsy and I came home and ate dinner.

BOOM….. Another panic attack hit me again. Heart racing, spinning, scared as ever again!! Ricoe took me back to the BHC (Breast Health Center) the nurse said that my breast which was just worked on looked fine. Nurse "M" helped me. She gave me some sprite to drink to help calm me down. She said I was just stressed! During all of this, my mom (Betty) just had rotator cuff surgery done on her left shoulder (5 torn places). My mom also has had double by-pass heart surgery! And I was just a wreck worrying about her as well as myself! God help us out! I am also worried about my baby D'Ara and how she is coping with us both of us being sick. D'Ara is at her dad's (Darnell) house and she wants to be at home. She understands but I feel bad because I can't help it. I want her home also. I continued to pray for my healing and the healing for others. It hasn't been easy but I'm making it through.

3-13-2009, NO CANCER IN LEFT BREAST!!! PRAISE GOD!

3-18-2009, I went to a Pain Management Class at the Cancer Center… Panic attack again … Stacy (nurse/manager) helped me through it. She taught me breathing methods and she set up an appointment for me to meet with Ms. Minna. My appointment with her is on next Thursday, 3-26-09. She felt that it was the stress as well. I'm trying to maintain it. Momma (Betty) checked my blood glucose (sugar) when I got home and it was 113! She said that was good!!

3-19-2009, I have to have surgery on both breasts, but I know God is Able! I am scheduled for pre-op on 4-8-09 and the surgery on 4-16-09. **But GOD!! I am going to make it I AM A SURVIVOR!!!!**

All family members and church members have been very supportive to me and my mom while we have been going through. I thank God for that everyday! Ricoe has been very wonderful and supportive to us as well! I thank God that he allowed him to come back into my life and be here for me as well as my friend, fiancée and partner. Janette also has been a very good help to us! Without her I don't know what I would do! She helped me with my momma so much. I thank God for her also! Considering she has her own illness and her husband (Jerry) illnesses! She's my rock and motivator! Thanks Janette!!

Ricoe and I went to the No One In The South Got Swagga Like Us Concert on 4-5-09 in Atlanta Ga. It was a very good concert. Ricoe and I had major fun. We stayed in Atlanta from Sunday to Tuesday just to get away before I have surgery. I had a panic attack again!! **I was scared as hell** but Ricoe calmed me down. He was very loving and caring and was there for me like never before. I am so happy and thankful to have him in my life!!! He helped to stop the panic attacks from going into full bloom! He eased my fears and pains and told me that he is here for me and not to worry everything's going to be alright! He was right. I made it through the night in his arms and in God's protections! **Thank God for Ricoe!!!**

On 4-8-09, I did pre-op for my breast lumpectomy at a hospital in Athens, Georgia. Mom and Ricoe took me to Dr. Gilbert's office to get the paperwork. They took me to the hospital for my pre-operation procedures. I stayed there from 1-4 pm. I was so tired and scared! I filled out a lot of paperwork.

I got my blood drawn twice plus I did a chest x-ray. I was scared about the x-ray!!

But God!!!! I was having another panic attack at the hospital because I was very nervous about having surgery and being put asleep. The nurse said that this is common for what I'm going through and what I am about to go through. I have been praying and worrying about my upcoming surgery on 4-10-09. I can't help it!! But God!! I know God will see me through!

4-10-2009, MORNING FOR BREAST CANCER SURGERY BY DR. GILBERT AT THE HOSPITAL AND DR. SCREVEN AT (BHC) BREAST HEALTH CENTER.

I was a total wreck…I was so scared and panicky. Mom and Ricoe dropped me off at the Breast Health Center where I was to get my needle localization, left breast biopsy and mammograms done. I arrived at the center around 8:30 that morning! I knew I was in for some rough stuff but little did I know it all turned out better than I ever could have imagined! All Praises is to God!!! I waited an hour before I was called to come to the back to get the needle localization done. I was freaking out because I had to wait so long. I met 2 nice ladies at the center while I waited. One lady told me she had been cancer free for 41 years and she had been where I was going and not to worry God has me. The other lady told me the same thing and that she would pray for me. They saw the scariness in my eyes and on my face. So finally, the time came for me to start my process: at 9:30 am the nurse did my localization with 8 shots to the right breast. The shots hurt like hell but the breast was numbed first. She was nice to me and helped me through it. Then, Loriana (ultrasound sonographer) came and got me and took me to take pictures of my left breast for biopsy. She then took pictures of my right breast. After waiting for a little while, she and Dr. Screven came back in my room. Dr. Screven said that she didn't like how my left breast looked still and that she wanted to be sure it had no cancer. She said I had to have both breasts needlized. I was crying and scared of course but I did what I had to do and prayed while they were working on my breasts.

Nurses Dawnetta, Loriana, Jeanna, and Michellea took mammogram pictures of both breasts after Dr. Screven placed the needles in both breasts. The needles hurt a little bit but I made it!!! **I WAS THINKING I AM SO READY FOR THIS TO BE OVER WITH!!!** Nurse Dawnetta was very helpful and she really tried to calm me down and make me laugh. Nurse Elisha hugged me and wished me well also. I was so happy to see her. I was taken to the hospital in a van through the side entrance by nurses Jeanna and Susana. They were so nice and kind and wheeled me to the hospital room to take a scan of the wires where the needles were. So this new nurse took the MRI pictures and finally around 12 noons or 12:30 she took me to the room to prepare for the major surgery by Dr. Gilbert. I was so happy to see my mom and Ricoe again!!!! Doris was there also with them. They thought that I was already done with the surgery but I was just getting started!!! I was wheeled to my room and my mom told me that she loved me and that I would be okay. Ricoe came in my room and helped me calm down because I was starting to panic again. I was starting to panic because they gave me more medicines. The medicines made my heart race and made me feel shaky like earlier before. My daddy, Pro, Mr. Uncle Ozzie, Jan, Shirley, and my best friend Ann all were there to visit me and support me. Ann and Ricoe had me tripping out and making my blood pressure machine go off!!!! They kept me laughing!!! My daddy also had me laughing and trying to calm me down before my surgery. I was still upset because it was so late and I still hadn't had the surgery. Dr. Gilbert came in and told me that he had 2 other emergency surgeries to perform before me. I was relieved then.

I didn't know what was going on. Nurse Loriana helped me out a lot while waiting for surgery. I had to be stuck twice again and I did not like it. The first nurse did not access my port right so Nurse Linda had to do it for me. I was so glad that God sent her in cause she cleaned my port plus showed the other Nurse how to use the port and what to do. She made me laugh and eased me through all the bad stuff I had to have done. All I remember is around 3:00 or 3:30 pm I felt panicky and nervous after being given Benadryl, Ativan, and other anesthesia medicines. My heart began to palpitate so Ricoe and the nurse calmed me down. Ricoe held my hand and told me not to worry he's here for me. I started to shake and feel nervous. I remember going with the nurse to the operating room and then from there it was over. The next thing I knew I was at home in my bed, eating around 9:00 p.m. and mom giving me my medicines and a bouquet of pretty rainbow roses in all colors….especially yellow (my favorite.) 1 Dozen of yellow, red, white, and pink roses… I took pictures and then I was out like a light!!!!

THANK GOD IT'S OVER!!! I MADE IT THROUGH BY THE GRACE OF GOD!!! THANK YOU GOD, MOMMA BETTY, RICOE, DR. GILBERT, DR. SCREVEN, AND MY DAUGHTER D'ARA.

One week later, 4-17-09, I had been very sore after my surgery, but I am glad that part is over with. PRAISE GOD!!!!!!

- ❖ I was cut in my left breast (side)
- ❖ Right Breast (bottom)
- ❖ Right Under Arm (nodes)
- ❖ Mole Removed (Right Breast)

I have taken plenty of Ibuprofen for pain and thanked God daily for his healing powers!!!! Thank you Jesus!!! I received the phone call on Tuesday, 4-14-09 around 4:00 p.m. from Nurse Practitioner Heather and she told me that the surgery went fine and that **I WAS CANCER FREE!!!! PRAISE GOD!!! NO MORE CANCER!!!! NO CANCER in left breast... CANCER gone in right breast... NO CANCER in lymph nodes.... MARGINS CLEAR... AINT GOD GOOD... YES HE IS!!!!** I was so happy and elated that I called my momma Betty right away. We were in Augusta, Georgia. Now I am just healing up from my surgery... waiting on my follow up doctor's appointment on 4-20-09 with Dr. Gilbert to see what's next for me.

4-20-09, I had my appointment with Dr. Gilbert after the surgery to get the stitches out. I was still a little sore. Dr. Gilbert and his nurse Denisha took them out. He said he was very happy with my progress and with my surgery going so well. He said I was all clear but I still needed to go through Radiation Therapy for 7 weeks. He also told me that the panic attacks were normal due to what I've been through and that it was going to get better. He made me an appointment to see Dr. Terrance for Radiation Therapy. Dr. Gilbert and his staff wished me well and I can visit whenever I wanted to or needed to.

MY JOURNEY CONTINUES...
NEXT PHASE...

5

FAITH

If u have faith the size of a mustard seed, you can say to this mountain be thou removed and it shall flee from you.

My faith was stretched beyond belief.

Only my belief and faith in God carried me.

I had the faith and now God said put your faith into action.

Will u trust me in this breast cancer battle?

While being stuck with needles constantly and feeling blue.

Faith was all I had and all I knew.

Some people speak of faith but never show it or use it.

I had to use and rely on my faith in God during this battle.

For the battle is His says the Lord and not mine.

Jesus promised never to leave me nor forsake me so faith was what helped me through.

4-23-09, my first visit to see Dr. Terrance to get set up for my Radiation treatments. This was a short visit because I didn't get to meet him. He had to leave for emergency surgery. I met his Nurse named Elena. She was very nice and sweet. We did all the necessary paperwork and she helped me to get ready to see Dr. Terrance for the next visit on tomorrow.

4-24-09, finally, met Dr. Terrance he seems really nice also. He said he liked my results from the surgery also. He examined me to get me measured for Radiation. He said I can start on Tuesday, 4-28-09. I was scared but God...his nurses Karana and Bettie got me ready for radiation. They took pictures, measured me, and marked me up with blue markers and clear tape. They had me in this MRI machine and all I could hear was loud noises. They were nice but I was tired because my right arm still hurt from the surgery. I had to get my "mold" right so I can receive the best radiation treatment for me. So, I laid there praying for them to mark me right so I can get going with the final part of my journey! My first Radiation treatment will be on Tuesday (4-28-09), I am a little nervous But God! He's never left me so I know He won't this time around either... Thank you Jesus!!

4-27-09, follow up appointment with Dr. Valdo. I saw Dr. Valdo and he said everything looked good and that he was pleased with my surgery and that I didn't need to take any pills and that he wanted to see me again in 3 months. He was happy with my progress so far!

4-28-09, First Radiation Treatment I was nervous just a little bit. I had all the glue marks on me so they would know where to start the radiation. I was praying as I laid on the radiation table my arms hurt a little especially the right one because it's still sore from the surgery. I wanted to move so badly but I had to lay still. The nurses were so nice to me by making sure I was aligned up right. (Karana, Bettie, and Michellea) the radiation stung my breast a little bit and the machine is very noisy and loud. It goes around and around about 3 times. I laid there for about a 1 ½ for the first day. It wasn't as bad as I thought. Just the laying down still and not being able to move is what I'm going to have to deal with! Thank God I made it this far!!!

Day Two was on 4-29-2009, this was a short treatment. It lasted for about 15 minutes! I was still up high on the machine and they had to try something new with my right breast today to make sure I was getting treated everywhere I needed to. They taped my right breast up to the machine to get a good treatment.

Day Three was on 4-30-2009, this was treatment number three. This was a good treatment and it was short also. Everything is going good so far.

Day Four was on 5-1-2009, this was treatment number four. This was also a short treatment. Everything is great as usual. Thank God for this!!!

May 1, 2009 --- I did the Relay for Life Walk ---- It was the Relay for Life Survivors Walk in Washington, Georgia. I walked with Uncle Willie Howard and Mr. Uncle Orzell Porter.

WE ARE TRULY PORTER SURVIVORS... We all hung out together this night. Momma Bet, Ricoe, D'Ara, Jessica, Macie, Uncle Raymond, Bessie "Betty Boo," Jeannette, "Uncle" Larry, Rozyln, Roger, Annie "Pie," and many others supported us as we did our survivors walk around the track. **We also remembered and did a memorial walk for Uncle Othar Porter (R.I.P.) - he died of Prostate Cancer on 2-17-2000. I love you and I miss you Uncle Othar – rest in peace. But God is Able.....**

Day Five was on 5-4-2009, this was treatment number five. It was a 20 minute treatment. Day Six was on 5-5-2009, this was treatment number six. This was a long and scary treatment. I had to go to a new room. I did not know what was going on. I had to be "molded" all over again!!! I was scared and about to have another panic attack but I did the breathing exercises to avoid the attack. I had to lay on the treatment table for over an hour. I was crying because I was scared and had to be moved to a new room. Nurses Karana and Juliana helped me through it. Juliana and Karana are so nice and sweet. They made sure everything was the way it was supposed to be. Every nurse in the Oncology department came in my room. This is why I was scared. **But God... I was so glad when it was over.** I saw Dr. Terrance and he said he was glad how my treatments were progressing.

Day Seven was on 5-6-2009, this treatment was number seven. Today was shorter and lasted for 20 minutes. I was so happy seeing how I stayed long yesterday. Day Eight was on 5-7-2009, this was treatment number eight. This treatment lasted for only 10 minutes. Praise God!!!! Day Nine was on 5-8-2009, this was treatment number nine. This treatment was also for about 10 minutes long. It was short and sweet. I did Relay for Life walk again. **I did the Relay for Life in Athens, Georgia. Donna, Anna, and I were together!!!! WE ARE SURVIVORS!!!!!!** I had fun with them just chilling out and hanging at the survivor's tent. We drunk some juice and just talked about how we were surviving our cancer thanks be to God Almighty up above!!!!

Day Ten was on 5-11-2009 this was treatment number ten. This was short and easy! It lasted for 10 minutes. I am getting used to my Radiation treatments better now!! THANK YOU JESUS!!! Day Eleven was on 5-12-2009 this was treatment number eleven. This was another scary day. I felt a panic attack trying to come on again. I did my breathing exercises and prayed to God as I lay on the table. **I was scared BUT GOD!!!!! TUESDAYS ARE MY TRYING DAYS!!! BUT I MAKE IT BY GOD'S GRACE AND MERCY!!!**

5-13-2009, Treatment, #12, now my treatments are starting to last longer since I'm in the new room. They're lasting 1 hour to over an hour. I'm scared but I want the nurses to get me treated right. As I lay on the table I pray for things to go right.

5-14- 2009, Treatment #13, this one lasted for at least an hour. Also I had to see Dr. Terrance today so he could check my skin progress out. He said my skin looked good. I am happy thanks to God!!!

5-15-09, Treatment #14, I'm now half-way done! Praise God!!! This treatment went very well! I'm getting used to putting the gel on everyday and every night! The gel is very sticky and sticks to my clothes!! But God!!! I did the Cancer Walk at D'Ara school on today also.

Monday 5-18-2009, Treatment #15, I got to the treatment late…As I already know when you're running late everything goes wrong... What I thought would be a 10-20 minute treatment turned into a 2 hour hectic long, scary, treatment! The nurses Michellea and Emilia could not for some reason line me up right on the table and take my pictures and X-rays right! All the nurses and doctors in the center had to help them. I was so scared and panicky and angry lying on the table for 1 hour. I was mad with Emilia and Michellea. I asked for Juliana and Karana to help calm me down. Juliana had to come and talk to me. I cried on her shoulders as she assured me Emilia and Michellea knew what they were doing and that they were only trying to make sure I was getting my treatment right. Nurses Kimona, Shayne, Elena, Bettie, Barbara, Juliana, and Karana all were helping to get me fixed up right! **I was so happy when it was over and I was off that table! Thank you Jesus!!!**

Tuesday, May 19, 2009, was treatment #16 and another long day of Radiation Therapy. Today was long like yesterday, but a little better. I had a new way of lining up on the table and it wasn't as difficult to line up for treatment!

I had to see Dr Terrance again today. He said he loved my progress and that my skin looked good and to continue to use the gel on it! He also apologized for the girls taking so long with me. He knew I was upset and nervous! He also recommended that I get my port in my arm checked and flushed! I asked Nurse Elena about it and she said it should be flushed every 4 to 6 weeks.

I went to the Cancer center today, walked in, and told the nurses I need my port flushed. I had to wait for 1 hour. I spoke with the social worker about some issues. I saw "Momma Geana," Geasha, Caria, Tracie, Charlotte, and a few others. They were glad to see that I was doing well and was feeling better. Nurse Dawnetta flushed out my port and told me it looked fine and to remember to get it flushed every 4-6 weeks.

Wednesday, May 20, 2009, Treatment #17, this treatment went smooth since I had my own "board" now. I had to get it taped all up like a Christmas present. I'm so special I have my own whole board. The nurses and I laughed so hard about my special board. The treatment was about 30 minutes. I was so happy things are going smooth again. A great treatment on today!!! PRAISE GOD! On after all I went through today, Nurse Elena told me my Cancer stage was Stage II a Breast Cancer...

Thursday, May 21, 2009, Treatment #18, this treatment went smooth also. It lasted for 30 minutes as well. Everything is still going smooth. Emilia and Michellea are getting better. Thank you Jesus for this!!!

Friday, May 22, 2009, Treatment #19, D'Ara went with me today to my treatment since nurses Karana, Juliana had been asking to see her. They all loved her and called her "mini me". They said she was cute and looked just like me. D'Ara took pictures of me getting treated. She loved this. This treatment was short, sweet, and fun. We joked again about my special board! Shayne came in and showed me how he did **"my duct tape" (the color of it was gray).** We all took pictures and joked around about my board. We laughed until we cried! It was so fun! This was the best treatment yet I think Praise God everything is still going great for me and my treatments. D'Ara and I hung out all day together!! **We just had Mother and daughter fun! Thank God for my daughter D'Ara!!! GO D'ARA...**

No treatment on Monday May 25, 2009 it would be a long holiday break for MEMORIAL DAY!!! Thank God for our VETERANS!!! R.I.P. to all those who've gone on to Glory with God!

Tuesday, May 26, 2009 was treatment number 20. This treatment went by fast. 20 minutes and it was over. It was the fastest treatment yet .... I think... All praises is to God!!!

Wednesday, May 27, 2009, was treatment number 21. This treatment took 20 minutes also. I am so happy the treatments are going smoother again!!! Thank you Jesus!!! Today is also my mom's 62nd birthday! She had to go to the emergency room for acid reflux. I stayed there with her for four hours. Thank God it was not her heart again!!! Just Acid Reflux...

Thursday, May 28, 2009, was treatment number 22. This treatment was also for only 20 minutes long. I had to see Dr. Terrance again today. He was still happy with my progress. He said my skin looked good. I was concerned about the tiny marks on my face. He said it was probably from the chemotherapy and that I didn't need to worry it looked alright to him. He told me to keep up the good work with my skin!!! Only 14 more treatments to go!!!!

Friday, May 29, 2009, was treatment number 23. This treatment was about 20 minutes long like usual. It was short and went great!!! But sad news hit the church family today….. One church family member died of **Cancer…. R.I.P. (W.F.M.)… YOU FOUGHT A GOOD FIGHT AND ALWAYS ENCOURAGED ME…. I KNOW YOU'RE IN HEAVEN NOW SMILING DOWN ON ME AND TELLING ME…"TARA HOLD ON"**

God help sustain his family and all of us who are fighting this thing called **CANCER.** Sunday, May 31, 2009 this was a very trying day for me. I had another crying spell plus a "mini" panic attack. I attended church which was dynamic of course. It was Pentecost Sunday! Day of Holy Ghost!!!

We buried our church member today after church at Clifford Grove Baptist Church in Rayle, Georgia. I guess I was so saddened by this loss that it really hit home for me after the funeral. I was sad, crying, panicky, and all. I had a dizzy spell going on and I just lay in bed after church and cried. Ricoe comforted me through this. He was truly there for me and I thank God for him again!!!!

Monday, June 1, 2009 was treatment number 24. Barbara and Michellea did my set up today. Barbara was very nice. She helped dressed my wounds under my right breast. She told me how to keep it from "breaking down." I thank God for her also! This treatment went fast! I was down again today in my spirits but God!!! The nurses told me to just relax and think on good things and that I'd be alright and YES it's normal for me to feel this way sometimes. I also spoke with Lois and she gave me some encouraging words too. Lois told me that I'm just feeling down because of one of our church members being gone but God is able to and that he's using me in this breast cancer situation not to fear or worry because God has me in his arms and in this place, at this time, for a reason and that all sickness is not unto death. I thank you God for life, health and strength as well as it is!!! And I know you're my Healer, Deliverer, and my ALL!!! THANKS FOR HAVING ME JESUS!!! AMEN!!!!

Tuesday, June 2, 2009, was treatment number 25. This treatment went by pretty fast. Karana and Michellea set me up today. This treatment burned my skin a lot. Karana blew cool air on my breast for me to stop the burning. She is a real sweet nurse. I had to see Dr. Terrance again today. He said my breasts needed to get some air especially the right breast. He said my skin was starting to burn to bad. So he gave me Wednesday and Monday off. He gave me some new cream medicines to put on my breasts for after treatment only. It helped my breasts feel a whole lot better. Dr. Terrance and Nurse Elena examined me and checked me out.

Wednesday, June 3, 2009 was not a good day for me. I did enjoy my day off but I think I got to hot in the sun. I was tired and feeling nauseous. I had a migraine headache all night plus I was running to the bathroom with diarrhea. I had another crying spell also. I do not know what is going on with me but I know that God is able…

Thursday, June 4, 2009 I WAS VERY SICK TODAY… I had to call and cancel my radiation treatment. I spoke with Nurse

Elena and she told me that it was okay to miss treatment today and to get better. I had a BAD MIGRAINE HEADACHE plus running with DIARRHEA AGAIN TODAY. I took an Ibuprofen and went to bed. I stayed in bed all day long. I was just not feeling good at all. I guess I am going through again. Ricoe is acting up; momma is tripping so I'm just not good at all. D'Ara is with her dad to prepare for her trip to Las Vegas on Monday. But God!!!!

Friday, June 5, 2009 was treatment number 26. This treatment went by fast. I had an early morning treatment at 8:20 am. It lasted for 30 minutes. Today I am feeling much better. Mom, Ricoe, and I are going to Savannah and Statesboro, Georgia for Ricoe's sister wedding renewal of 19 years of marriage. We left after I did my treatments. Friday night in Savannah, we went to the malls and hung out. The malls were a little different than the Athens, Georgia mall. We ate at a Seafood Restaurant. Fresh cooked fish and shrimp – mmh, mmh, and mmh good. I couldn't wait for this. I love this good shrimp. Ricoe took me to see his old house in Rincon, Georgia after 14 years.

Saturday, June 6, 2009 was the Wedding Renewal of 19 years in Statesboro, Georgia. It rained so hard mostly all day long. The wedding renewal was good and funny. The Pastor kept messing up on their vows. He was more nervous than bride and groom was. I met Ricoe's dad Landis for the first time today also. I felt that Ricoe and his dad looked just like twins!!! After the wedding renewal, we went downtown Savannah to River Street. We went to to the Bar and it was fun!!!! We tried the drinks... "Catch a cab", "Strawberry daiquiri," Monkey shine," and "Blue motherfucker." We got "fucked up!!!" The "catch a cab" drink was very strong. One hit and I was about high. LOL… We had a good time just walking on River Street. We went to the candy factory also. I saw how they made Laffy taffy candy. On Sunday morning, June 7, 2009 we ate breakfast at

Mama Shirley's house before we left to return home to Athens, Georgia. Ricoe and I had a good talk tonight and on Sunday about our relationship. I praise God for him even in our ups and downs… He is staying home for a week with his mother in South Carolina. We returned home on Sunday, June 7, 2009 around 5:00 p.m.

Monday, June 8, 2009 was treatment number 27. It was a longer treatment. It lasted for about 40 minutes. Karana, Juliana, and Emilia set me up today. I had to be set up 3x today!!! "I TOOK IT LIKE A CHAMP!!!!!" I was tired but I know I have to keep going. The board was a little off today. Karana fanned me again because my breasts burned a lot. Juliana says it looks okay but will check with Nurse Elena on tomorrow plus let Dr. Terrance look at my skin tomorrow. They told me that these treatments were supposed to have my breasts looking like this. I hurt a lot under my breasts but I am pressing on. I used the cream/gel right after each treatment now. I am supposed to start a new treatment set up on Wednesday for the final 8 treatments. I pray that these go well… Thank you God for where you have brought me so far!!! Amen!!!! D'Ara left for Las Vegas today with her dad Darnell and Grandma Doris.

Tuesday, June 9, 2009 today is treatment number 28. Today was another 30-40 minute treatment. My breasts really hurt and were burning a lot. The right breast especially. It is very black and starting to bleed and breakdown. Dr. Terrance says my skin needs to take a break. He gave me until Monday off so my skin can rest. Nurse Elena gave me some medicines and pads to cover my breasts with for the week until Monday. The medicines felt very good. Nurses Elena and Karana helped me with my skin!!! I will start the new treatments on Monday where they will focus on where the cancer was under my breasts. Thank you God for continued healing of my breasts….

Wednesday, June 10, 2009 to Friday, June 12, 2009

I had days off so my skin could rest and sort of heal again. I kept the medicines on my breasts as Dr. Terrance told me too. The medicines were called Silver Med. This medicine feels real good and helps out a lot.

THURSDAY, JUNE 11, 2009 I BOUGHT ME ANOTHER HONDA ACCORD CAR. I BOUGHT A 1998 HONDA ACCORD LX (IT'S SILVER). THANK YOU JESUS FOR MY CAR!!! IN MY OWN NAME FOR EVERYTHING!!! PRAISE GOD!!!!!!

I first drove my car home on Monday, June 15, 2009 which was D'Ara's 10th birthday!!! Today was treatment number 29. This treatment was long and scary!! It was the new treatment. I was having a panic attack. I prayed hard and did the breathing treatments while on the radiation table. My breasts hurt so badly. They are really black now and I hate how they look but I thank God that I am **ALIVE**. PRAISE GOD!!! Karana, Juliana, and Michellea helped me through the day. Thank you God I made it through. We celebrated D'Ara's 10th birthday at an Italian Restaurant!!! We went to the mall, and to various other stores. D'Ara and Macie got their nails done at the nail shop. This was D'Ara's first time getting her fingernails and toes done. She had real fun!! Mom, Doris, Macie, Leemarcus, Ariana, and I helped to celebrate D'Ara's birthday. D'Ara and I hung out all day long for her birthday!!! I am glad we celebrated her day and I was able to be with her to celebrate it!!!

HAPPY 10TH BIRTHDAY D'ARA

Tuesday, June 16, 2009 this is treatment number 30. D'Ara came to treatment with me again today. This went very quickly. D'Ara and I had fun with the ladies again today. They were so happy to see her again. She watched me again as I took my treatment. This one was very short today. Thank you Jesus!!! My breasts stung a little bit but I made it!! I saw Dr. Terrance today and he gave me 1 day off!! My breasts still breaking down to new skin!! The medicines feel good on my breasts plus the air on them feels good too.

Ricoe came back home on today also. Ricoe brought his son back with him on today also. His son came to spend the summer with us. Thank you Jesus!!! Amen!!!! **6 more treatments to go!!!** Wednesday, June 17, 2009 was my day off…

Thursday, June 18, 2009 this was treatment number 31. This treatment went by pretty fast. It was about 30 minutes long. The treatment still stings my breasts but I pray while I am on the table and it's over before I know it. Karana, Juliana, and Michellea always help me by easing my mind. I thank God for them in my life!! I met with the social worker Mamie at the Cancer Center. Mamie is real nice. She tried to get me help with other housing options other than where I am staying now. She also gave me free parking passes again… Praise Jesus!!! I will make it… you've never left me before and I know you won't leave me now!!!!

Friday, June 19, 2009 this was treatment day number 32. I had an "early bird treatment." I was the first one at 8:00 a.m. It lasted for about 20 minutes. Karana and Michellea set me up for treatment today. This treatment burned just a little bit. I made it through okay though. Ricoe and I hung out in Atlanta all day with our kids. We went to a mall in Atlanta, Georgia. It was good. Thank God for another blessed day. **4 more treatments to go!!!**

Monday, June 22, 2009 this was treatment day number 33. This treatment went really fast just like the others. Thank you Jesus!! Karana and Michellea set me up again today. I didn't feel any burning today Praise God!!! Michellea said my skin was healing up like it is supposed to be. I am very happy about that. I am very happy about that!!!!

Tuesday, June 23, 2009 this was treatment number 34. Today was a good treatment day. I surprised the Radiation team with fruit, cookies, and juice. They were so surprised and happy. They all signed my journal book for me and wished me well. My skin was beginning to heal very well. I am continuing to use the medicines and they are helping to heal my skin. I was so hyped up for the little party ... The party went well but, **then BOOM....**

Mama called me and told me to stay at the hospital because they were bringing D'Ara up there because her blood sugar was 489. I was so scared because she had already been sleeping a lot, losing weight, and just not looking right to me. Mama, Darnell, Doris, and a friend, and I were there at the hospital with her. They ran plenty of tests on D'Ara and her blood glucose levels still did not come down. I was scared, sad, crying, and all. The doctors decided that D'Ara needed to go to Atlanta to the Children's Hospital to get help with her diabetes. **The doctor confirmed that she did indeed have Type 1 Juvenile Diabetes.** I rode in the ambulance with her and I mostly cried all the way there. I was praying and making phone calls to get prayer for her and me. I was truly a wreck but I knew that God is able... I was glad that I was nearly done with my cancer radiation treatments. D'Ara was very sick this day!! But she knew that she would be okay. She learned to give herself a shot to check her blood sugars. She also learned how to give herself insulin medicine that she would need.

Wednesday, June 24, 2009, this is day two at the Children's Hospital in Atlanta with D'Ara. Darnell, D'Ara, and I took the first day diabetic class. We learned how to check her blood sugar, how to give her insulin, how to count her carbohydrates, how to count ketones, how to tell low and high blood sugars, how to keep her exercises regulated, and all medical information she needed. D'Ara and I had alone time together. It was much needed since I had been sick with my breast cancer but now the role is reversed. We still enjoyed our time together… We watched a movie, went to the library, we did artwork, we played cards, we played games. We did mother and daughter things while at the hospital. Today is my Aunt Mary "Sua" birthday. Mia, Ann, Aunt Mary "Sua", and Ge'Mia came to visit us at the hospital. We went to Bible Study. D'Ara, Ann, Michelle, her mom Teresa and I went to this bible study. Michelle and Teresa were two people D'Ara and I had met at the diabetic class and hospital. **The topic for bible study was on STRUGGLES!!!!!** How is it that in this time in my life God knew just what I needed when I needed it? He's an on time God… Yes he is!!!! The speaker was Mrs. Wilhelmina. **She spoke on how we should turn our struggles over to JESUS… and he'll work them out for us.** She read from the scriptures of Psalms 18 and Psalms 9. "I will sing praise to your name, O God. I will trust in you. I will turn to you. I will lean on you. I will remember and not forget that you are everlasting to everlasting." She spoke to D'Ara and Monique and encouraged them about their newly diagnosis of diabetes. She told them to pray to Jesus to heal them and lean on him. She song the song "Lean on Me" and encouraged us to lean on Jesus in this time in our lives. This service was good!!! Amen!!!!

D'Ara's blood sugars went up and down. The medicines have to get time to work. The doctors told us to expect changes like this in her sugar levels. We have to check her blood sugars at 2am in the morning. I am very panicky but I know God is able. I just lay there and prayed to God to heal my baby D'Ara and to continue to heal me also. **I know we must have GREAT WORK TO DO FOR JESUS BECAUSE THESE "SICKNESS DEMONS" ARE BUSY IN OUR LIVES...BUT WE ARE HEALED BY HIS STRIPES... IT IS SO!!!!**

Thursday, June 25, 2009 is day two of classes for Dee, D'Ara, and I. We learned to count carbohydrates, read labels, do the heart rate, plus do exercises with D'Ara. D'Ara played bingo, did artwork, watched movies, hung out with the child life staff, and made a diabetic bracelet. D'Ara is feeling better today and she also was released to go home from the hospital. **PRAISE GOD!!! CONTINUED HEALING OF D'ARA... I was very overwhelmed today trying to count carbohydrates, give insulin, and make sure everything for D'Ara was going okay.** Darnell, D'Ara, and I rode home together today... on the way home I got sad news.... Three good people I know **ALL PASSED AWAY TONIGHT.... BUT GOD!!! THANK GOD WE HAVE ANOTHER CHANCE TO GIVE HIM THE PRAISE!!! D'ARA is home and we are managing her diabetes.**

I was sick with a migraine headache from all of this stress, but by God's grace and mercy I am going to make it!!! I had to take an Ibuprofen when I finally did get home. I called my cousin a million times I know to get some help and ideas since her and her son are already going through what D'Ara and I are now facing. She has been a good help to me and her son a good help to D'Ara. Thank you Jesus all prayers are being answered. D'Ara's blood sugar levels are getting regulated.

Friday, June 26, 2009, was treatment number 35. This treatment went very fast. It only lasted for about 30 minutes. Everyone was asking how D'Ara and I were doing. The staff was very nice to me today and throughout this whole process of my radiation. They were glad that D'Ara was home and that I could finally finish my last 2 radiation treatments......

Monday, June 29, 2009 WAS MY FINAL DAY OF RADIATION THERAPY..... Treatment number 36. This treatment took about and 1hour or more to finish. **THIS WAS MY GRADUATION DAY... I WAS SO HAPPY AND EXCITED ABOUT FINALLY BEING FINISHED WITH IT ALL..... PRAISE GOD I MADE IT ALL THE WAY THROUGH BY HIS GRACE AND MERCY ONLY DID I DO IT.....** The staff and I cried as I was finishing up and about to leave. We were happy that I was finishing up but it was still sad that we would not see each other every day no more as usual. I will miss the Radiation team: Karana, Juliana, Michellea, Emilia, Kim, Shayne, Keyana, Tracie, Bettie, Elena, Doctor Terrance, and Barbara.

On Monday, July 13, 2009, I went to my follow up appointment with Dr. Terrance at the Radiation Department. He said that my breasts looked good and that my skin was healing fine.... I still praise God for this healing process...

On Monday, July 20, 2009, I went to the Cancer Center for my follow up appointment with Dr. Valdo. He was not there so I saw his Nurse Practitioner Ms. K. She was very happy with how far I had come with fighting this breast cancer. She said everything looked great and that I could see Dr. Valdo in six more months then I'd get my port taken out. I told her of my concern with my menstrual cycle still not coming back on yet. She suggested that I make an appointment to see a gynecologist. So, I asked for suggestions on gynecologists who would take Medicaid. I was given several doctors name as suggestions.

On Monday, July 27, 2009 I had my port removed at the hospital. Ricoe took me to the hospital to get this procedure done. On the way there, I constantly told him of how scared I was. He assured me that I would be okay. This was another scary day for me. I was having another panic attack moment. I was scared of all of the medicine I had to take to get the port taken out. I am allergic to a lot of medicine so I was scared when the nurses came to give me medicine. I was given Ativan again to relax plus Benadryl and Morphine. I was a little bit sleepy but not a lot. I was awake while the port was being taken out. I heard the nurses and doctors talking to me while doing the procedure. One male nurse was very good to me in the operating room. He rubbed my head while the procedure was taking place. He let me know that I was going to be alright. He assured me that it would go smoothly. Ricoe helped me through this day also. He was very good with me and also told me not to worry. After the procedure, I ate my food, took my medicines, and went to bed. **PRAISE GOD I HAD MY PORT REMOVED OUT SAFELY!!!**

Also in the month of July, I finally was fitted for a prosthetic bra by Ms. Christina. I was stunned and shocked to know that I wear a size 38F. (LOL) I was always wearing a size 38D. It was real fun getting my bra fitting done. I learned a lot about bra sizing and fitting after having to go through all this breast cancer stuff.

September 1, 2009 was the day I finally saw a gynecologist about my menstrual cycle. I saw the doctor and his staff. He was a great gynecologist. He was very nice and assured me that everything would be okay again. I explained to him what had happened during my chemotherapy and during my breast cancer fight. He felt that my cycle had left due to chemotherapy. He did the normal Pap smear and pelvic exam tests. He said my cycle should return again soon. The gynecologist turned out to be right.......

My menstrual cycle returned after being gone for nearly a year on September 5, 2009 while I was at Daytona Beach Florida. I was happy and sad all at the same time. I was in Daytona Beach celebrating being Breast Cancer free and boom that happened...Lol.... Mother Nature knows when to strike huh.... Overall Ricoe and I still had fun at Daytona Beach Florida for Labor Day weekend. We went to the malls, to the Flea Markets, and to the shops on the Beach. We walked the beach at night and celebrated my upcoming one year Breast Cancer Freedom....

September 15, 2009, I did an interview with a journalist of a magazine to share my Breast Cancer story for the upcoming Breast Cancer Month (October 2009). I freely share my Breast Cancer experience to inspire, encourage, and educate all women to help them have the desire to fight and not give up and to want to continue to live.

ONE YEAR CANCER FREE 9-17-2009

September 17, 2009 MARKS MY ONE YEAR OF BEING BREAST CANCER FREE......... I celebrated by visiting the staff of the Cancer Center, and the Breast Health Center staff. They were all so happy that I had made my ONE YEAR MARK. Both staffs were so happy and pleased with my progress. Ricoe cooked me a celebration dinner. He cooked steak, some potatoes, prepared a salad and some rice for my celebration dinner. I put my one year photo on my internet page to share with the world my happiness and joy of being BREAST CANCER FREE FOR ONE YEAR... ALL PRAISES GO TO GOD UP ABOVE FOR WITHOUT HIM I TRULY NEVER WOULD HAVE MADE IT!!!!! I also shared my one year celebration story on the breast cancer site website page. It can be viewed at this web address:http://www. thebreastcancersite.com/clickToGive/photostory.faces? siteId=2&storyTag=fzkft4kb1u8ulhvdladds&confirmation Code=n0h5mt0emc9q.

My Journey with fighting Breast Cancer---1 year survivor---

Share your inspirational survivor or supporter story with others

Read more stories!

My Journey with fighting Breast Cancer---1 year survivor---

I started having lumps in my breasts when I was 15 and started my menstrual cycle. The lumps would come and go away each month. But in July 2009, the lump in my right breast did not go away. I scheduled myself a mammogram appointment after seeing a doctor about my breasts. I had my mammogram done and sadly to say on 9-17-08 I was diagnosed with Stage II A Breast Cancer at the age of 34. I had chemotherapy treatments done, two lumpectomies done in my right and left breasts, lymph nodes taken out of my right arm (surgery), 36 radiation treatments ...But by the grace of God, prayers from family, friends, and church family I made it through. James 5:16 help me to be a Breast Cancer Survivor.... "Pray ye one for another, that you may be healed." In my time of sickness, I prayed for others with this same disease and other sicknesses and God healed me. Special thanks to my mom, Betty, daughter D'Ara, and fiancé Ricoe... I love you guys so much.... September 17, 2009 marks my 1 year of being Breast Cancer Free....Praise God!!! Amen!!! Tara Thomas, Athens, Georgia

October 7, 2009, I went for my six month annual mammogram and follow up appointment at the Breast Health Center in Athens, Georgia. The appointment was a little scary. It was like starting all over again. I knew that I was already CANCER FREE, but it is still scary going to get your mammogram done. The entire time I was waiting to get my mammogram done, little thoughts came in my head, yet I know God is able. I took the mammogram and it hurt like hell. I had my breasts squeezed so hard in the machine. I had to pray literally while getting it done. My breast (right) is still a little sore from all that has been done to it. I always feel a sting to my right breasts and it hurts. The nurses say that this stinging feeling is normal. It comes from the radiation treatments. The sting is unbearable at times and unexplainable. MY RESULTS WERE… I AM STILL CANCER FREE AND DOING WELL. PRAISE GOD!!!!! I met with Nurses Emilia and Michellea about my upcoming program scheduled for October 24, 2009 for Breast Cancer Awareness and shared my good news from my mammogram report. They were happy for me!!!

On the weekend of October 24 – 25, 2009, I had a WORSHIP IN PINK… PASSIONATELY PINK WEEKEND PROGRAM FOR BREAST CANCER AWARENESS. I had these programs to educate women and men on the importance of having mammograms done. I wanted to share about Breast Cancer Awareness. I wanted to share my personal healing from CANCER!!!!

I had these programs at Macedonia Baptist Church and Clifford Grove Baptist Church. It was a learning experience for me as well as others. Many cancer survivors attended my program and shared their testimonials of how God healed them of their cancer as well. In closing, I want to sum up this journey of fighting breast cancer by saying its all in whom you believe in and that is **GOD ALMIGHTY UP ABOVE**. I pray that you have been blessed and inspired to change your life and to have a personal relationship with Christ. If you do not have one I urge you to make Christ your lord and savior. I also want you to be aware of your body and the changes your body goes through. I encourage women to have a mammogram done and to do self breast exams monthly it will save your life just as it did mine. May God forever bless you and keep you in his care. When nothing else is left, just believe.

6

BELIEVE

If only you can believe it you can do it.
I believed that I could come out of Breast Cancer.
I felt at times like it was over but I thought back to harder struggles and how I made it.
I felt like Jesus did not bring me this far to leave me.
He had his plans for my life in allowing me to go through Breast Cancer.
Now I know and honestly I can say that I believe it was to make me stronger.
What doesn't kill you only makes you stronger.
I know this now.
Just believe and God will do the rest.
When nothings left to do just BELIEVE.....

7

LOVE

I loved myself enough to battle this thing called BREAST
CANCER.
Love is of God and God is Love.
My family and friends showed me love.
God's love covered me everyday I battled
Breast Cancer.
Love is showing action not feelings.
Show love one to another by praying for each other.
"Pray ye one for another that you may be healed." James 5:16

Love shown by my family and friends......

The Radiation Therapy Team Well Wishes

"It was a pleasure getting to know you. I wish you the best. May god continue to bless you. Let me know if you need anything else built." (The board for radiation) Love, (Shayne)

"That crazy bag. Just for you. (A special person needs a special bag). "It was such a pleasure to know. You have been an inspiration. Take care of yourself."

Love, Ms. (Emilia)

"God is with you always." Love, Ms. (Bettie)

Congrats Girl "You Did Dat." It was wonderful getting to know you. Love, Ms. (Keyana)

"I am blessed to know you. I know that god will use this for you to bless others. Let your light shine!" God bless you! (Elena)

"Congrats! You did it! You have been a joy to know you." Love, Ms. (Tracie)

"I have really enjoyed talking to you each day. You are a special girl and I wish the best." Take care, Michellea

"I have really enjoyed working with you. You rock!" Doctor (Terrance)

"You have been a trooper through all of this and a pleasure to be around. Your smile lights up the department!" Love, Ms. Kimona

"I can't begin to tell you how awesome that you did. From the first day from then on you had to put up with crazy me. I enjoyed your smile everyday even though it seemed like we took our time. Please take care of that beautiful little girl and your self. Keep god first in your life and you can do anything. You made it girl- Save the Ta-Ta's! I will miss seeing you but stop by to say hello." Take care. Karana

"Well who will I "high five" with when you finish up here?? I can't believe you won't be here everyday to make us laugh, but I am so happy for you. It takes a truly strong and a brave woman to take on any situations with such faith and courage. You are true inspiration to us all and I hope that one day you'll be there for us if we need you... I'll never forget you and your smiling face and faith in god and his plan for us all... God bless you and yours Juliana "Holla Back"

"Make sure you keep us updated when you finish. You better not forget us because we won't forget you! You are so special to think of us while you are going through all this. It has really been a pleasure getting to know you." Take care & God bless. Barbara

Chemotherapy Staff of the Cancer Care Center Well Wishes

"Love this girl. She's my sweet adopted daughter. May god bless you and you and your family." Love you, Ma Geana

"Tara I am so glad that you are done with (chemo.) I am so glad that I was there with you. Thank the lord for our friendship. May god bless and keep you safe" Love, Ms. Penelope

"To a very special person god have lead you that he will not leave you stay close to him and keep reading Psalms 27 1-6 everyday." Love, Ms. Geasha

"To a very special and sweet, young woman whom can do all things through Jesus Christ who strengthen her." Love, Ms. Patricia P.S. Think positive and look to the Lord

"Tara you've done good! I'm so proud of you. It's been a pleasure working with you! Good luck with everything!" Always, Jill Clark

Kimberly, NP-C, AOCNP

"God bless you and keep you." Much Love, Catria Farrar

"May God continue to bless you and I'll keep you in my prayers." Love, Ms. Coco (from the Pharmacy)

"May the Lord continue to bless you with good health." Love, Ms. Browner

"God continues to smile on you." Best wishes, Ms. Richardson

"May God continue to bless you and your family." Love, Vanessa

"May God keep you and protect you always." Be blessed, Charlotte

Dr. Gilbert and Staff Well Wishes

Kara says "Good luck to you"

Heather says "Best of luck Tara! You are an inspiration to all of us."

Simona says "Best of wishes and good luck"

My family and friends well wishes

"May god keeps blessing you and keep god first in your life." Love your daughter, D'Ara Thomas

"Get well soon! Take care and fell much better." Kennae Hunter

"I know god was on your side and keep on praying and putting him first in everything you do." Love your Mom, Betty Booker

"Hope you get well so we can do what we like to do." I love you. Tika Chapman 2009

"Tara you are the best and I love you for life." Your big Sister, Gale Hurley

Georgia Mae Faust, Janie Campbell, Marquis D. Jones

Brit Stewart says "Love you! Keep on Living!"

"To my sister I love you very, very much and best wishes." Your sister, Evangelist Lisa Perlotte

"To my sis and cuz Tara I love you and let god use you to the fullness." Love, Jenny Young

"Love you! Bless you! The best big sister in the whole wide world!" Love, Deshonda Turner

"Hi. Tara, when I first heard that you had Breast Cancer. I really felt so sad about it, but I put it in God's hands, God can cure EVERYTHING." Love, Janette Smith

BREAST HEALTH CENTER WELL WISHES

For my 1 year Anniversary (9-17-09)

"God bless you on your anniversary hope you have many more." Jolenea

"God bless you. Go forward in God."

Yvette

"We are all so happy to celebrate 1 year of victory. We're here for you many, many more. You are such an inspiration!" Dr. Screven

"Thanks for your beautiful spirit! Happy 1 Year!!! All the best!! Elizabetha

"We are so happy you're doing well!!"

Mistiana

"We are so happy for you! Congrats!! You are such an inspiration!! Dawnetta

"We are so glad you are doing so well. You look great!! I am very proud to see you doing so well!! Loriana

REFERENCES

Bible verses from King James Version Bible©

Health Centers and Hospitals:

Cancer Center in Athens, Georgia
Hospital in Athens, Georgia
Breast Health Center in Athens, Georgia
Cancer Care Center in Athens, Georgia
Radiation Oncology Department in Athens, Georgia

About Me...
The Author...Just Tara

My name is Tara La'Shawn Porter Thomas. I am a 42 year old female with two daughters. My daughter's names are D'Ara Thomas and Morgan Paul. My mother's name is Betty Ann Booker. My father's name is Johnny Stephens Jr. I am a member of the Clifford Grove Baptist Church in Rayle, Georgia. I love writing poetry, taking pictures, using the computer, and just hanging out with my family and friends. I am a very happy person. I love to joke around and have fun. My nickname is Shorty. I love to work with children. I have worked with children on various jobs as a teacher, mentor, paraprofessional, and counselor all of my life. Due to my sickness, I had to stop working. Through my love of computers, God gave me the vision of a business which was called **Just Tara's Touch Typing** back in 1998. In this business, I would do computer work such as type programs, cards, reports, invitations, and etc...

Later on, I expanded my vision and business and added photography to it. I love to take pictures so I started doing photography for friends and family. Little did I know that the business would keep expanding and lead me to where I am today? **Just Tara's Touch Pink.** I was diagnosed with Stage II A Breast Cancer on September 17, 2008. I thought that I was too young to have breast cancer at the age of 34, but God... God gave me the vision again to Just Tara's Touch... now **Just Tara's Touch Pink** which stands for Touching Others Using my Cancer Healing for People In Need of Knowledge about Breast Cancer... (T.O.U.CH. P.I.N.K.) He showed me in my dreams where I was to go out and share with the nation his healing power of my body from Breast Cancer to all people (especially young women) and he would bless me more. So I am writing this book to inspire, to encourage, and to declare God's glory and healing power to all. May the words in this book touch you like never before. Be Blessed!!!

Just Tara's Touch Pink Founder, Tara L. Thomas
7 years Breast Cancer Survivor